# 21 Day

## Prayer Challenge:
## Steps to doing it God's way

### Prayer Journal

## APOSTLE PEGGY RATLIFF

**21 DAY PRAYER CHALLENGE: STEPS TO DOING IT GOD'S WAY,** is a comprehensive guide for individuals seeking to deepen their prayer life and build a closer relationship with God. This prayer journal presents a 21-day challenge where readers are given a specific task to complete each day.

Some of the topics covered in the prayer journal include, "Examine Your Heart", "A Day of Thanksgiving and Praise", "A Heart to Heart Talk with God", "How to Surrender in Prayer", "Pray for Your Enemies", and more. Each of these topics is relevant to everyday life and provides practical insights for how to pray effectively.

This guide's simple yet effective structure, insightful commentaries, and thought-provoking questions, make it a must-have for anyone looking to grow in their faith.

**PEGGY RATLIFF**

It is through our challenges that we begin to mature and grow.

PEGGY RATLIFF

# RECOGNIZING GOD'S VOICE IN YOUR LIFE...

"My sheep listen to my voice; I know them, and they follow me." John 10:27. Those who hear God's voice are those who belong to Him.

PEGGY RATLIFF

# RECOGNIZING GOD'S VOICE IN YOUR LIFE...

Perhaps you have struggled or are struggling with how God speaks to you personally. Developing a personal relationship with God can be unique sometimes. Therefore, it can be helpful to seek the guidance of trusted spiritual leaders or mentors who can offer support and insight as you explore your spiritual journey. For example, in I Samuel 3 the Lord was trying to talk to Samuel, however, he was having difficulty recognizing God's voice. Perhaps you can relate to him? Samuel therefore needed his mentor, Eli, to help him figure out what was happening. Therefore, do not give up, and do not be discouraged! If you do not already know how God speaks to you, you will learn!

**PEGGY RATLIFF**

# RECOGNIZING GOD'S VOICE IN YOUR LIFE...

There are many different ways that people can experience how God communicates with them. Here are some examples of ways that people might identify with how God speaks to them:

- Through prayer.
- Through scripture.
- Through others.
- Through ways you would not think.

PEGGY RATLIFF

# RECOGNIZING GOD'S VOICE IN YOUR LIFE...

## Through prayer...

Many people believe that **prayer** is a way to communicate with God, and that God can speak to us in response to our prayers. This might come in the form of a sense of peace, a feeling of guidance or direction, or even an answer to a specific question or concern.

# RECOGNIZING GOD'S VOICE IN YOUR LIFE...

**Through scripture...**

The reading of **scripture** can be a way to hear God's voice. Many believe that God speaks to them through His word and messages in Scripture, revealing new insights and guidance. (Joshua 1:8)

PEGGY RATLIFF

# RECOGNIZING GOD'S VOICE IN YOUR LIFE...

## Through others...

God can sometimes speak to us **through people**. It is where our faith in God comes alive because after you have prayed and waited on an answer from God, He sometimes sends His Prophet or just a servant to speak to us. God speaking to us also comes in the form of a life-changing sermon or message. For example, someone may send a scripture that speaks to your heart or situation. (Romans 10:17)

PEGGY RATLIFF

# RECOGNIZING GOD'S VOICE IN YOUR LIFE...

**Through ways you would not think...**

**God does not always speak to us the way** we expect Him to. Therefore, it is always helpful, when you seek God's guidance and wisdom in prayer, to take any expectations you have and throw them out the window. **He does not always move in the way** we expect Him to. Isaiah 55:8-9 tells us "For My thoughts are not your thoughts, neither are your ways My ways, declares the LORD. For as the heavens are higher than the earth, so My ways are higher than your ways and My thoughts than your thoughts". Understanding spiritual things requires spiritual discernment. This is why we need the Holy Spirit operating in our lives, to seek the will of God and to communicate with Him.

PEGGY RATLIFF

# 21 Day PRAYER CHALLENGE - REFLECTIONS

**Date:**

_____

_____

_____

_____

_____

_____

_____

_____

_____

_____

_____

_____

_____

_____

_____

_____

_____

_____

# 21 Day PRAYER CHALLENGE - REFLECTIONS

**Date:**

_____

_____

_____

_____

_____

_____

_____

_____

_____

_____

_____

_____

_____

_____

_____

_____

_____

# 21 Day PRAYER CHALLENGE - REFLECTIONS          Date:

_____

_____

_____

_____

_____

_____

_____

_____

_____

_____

_____

_____

_____

_____

_____

_____

# 21 Day PRAYER CHALLENGE - REFLECTIONS

Date:

_____

_____

_____

_____

_____

_____

_____

_____

_____

_____

_____

_____

_____

_____

_____

_____

_____

_____

# DAY 1 – EXAMINE YOUR HEART

*Scripture – I Samuel 16:7, "But the Lord said to Samuel, 'Do not consider his appearance or his height, for I have rejected him. The Lord does not look at the things people look at. People look at the outward appearance, but the Lord looks at the heart."*

There are times when our appearance is just a facade (an outward appearance that is maintained to conceal a less pleasant or creditable reality). It does not reflect who we truly are. The Lord does not see us from our outer appearance; He looks at our heart.

For our day one of our 21-day prayer challenge, ask God to reveal your heart. What does God see? David had to ask God to create in him a new heart and a right spirit. This is necessary, as believers and followers of Christ, for love is our trademark, and love is the heart of God. According to scripture, I Corinthians 13:4-8 says, "Love is patient, love is kind. It does not envy, it does not boast, it is not proud. It does not dishonor others, it is not self-seeking, it is not easily angered, it keeps no record of wrongs. Love does not delight in evil but rejoices with the truth. It always protects, always trusts, always hopes, always perseveres. Love never fails." Therefore, let us see what God will reveal to you!

**PEGGY RATLIFF**

# DAY 1 – EXAMINE YOUR HEART

## QUESTIONS

1. What did God reveal to you? How will you respond?

2. What did you learn new about yourself?

3. What blessed you most today?

# 21 Day PRAYER CHALLENGE - DAY 1    Date:

_____

_____

_____

_____

_____

_____

_____

_____

_____

_____

_____

_____

_____

_____

_____

_____

# 21 Day PRAYER CHALLENGE - DAY 1    Date:

_____

_____

_____

_____

_____

_____

_____

_____

_____

_____

_____

_____

_____

_____

_____

_____

# 21 Day PRAYER CHALLENGE - DAY 1    Date:

_____

_____

_____

_____

_____

_____

_____

_____

_____

_____

_____

_____

_____

_____

_____

# 21 Day PRAYER CHALLENGE - DAY 1     Date:

_____

_____

_____

_____

_____

_____

_____

_____

_____

_____

_____

_____

_____

_____

_____

_____

God, examine me and know my heart; test me and know my anxious thoughts. See if there is any bad thing in me. Lead me on the road to everlasting life.

Psalm 139:23-24

# DAY 2 – A DAY OF THANKSGIVING AND PRAISE

*Scripture – Psalm 100:4, "Enter into his gates with thanksgiving, and into his courts with praise: be thankful unto him, and bless his name."*

On this day before the Lord, during your time of prayer, give thanks to the Lord and praise Him. This is not synonymous with supplication prayers where you ask God to meet your needs. Instead, this is a day that is about who God is, and what He has already done. So, as you seek His face, bless His holy name, worship Him with songs, and allow your heart to be filled up with gratitude! Next, share with at least one person about the goodness of the Lord in your life. Then, end your day reflecting on all that occurred, and meditate on the following scriptures: Psalm 136:1 says, "Oh give thanks unto the Lord; for he is good: for his mercy endureth forever. Psalm 107:2 says, "Let the redeemed of the Lord say so, whom he hath redeemed from the hand of the enemy." Psalm 92:2 says, "To shew forth thy lovingkindness in the morning, and thy faithfulness every night." Cleary, these bible scriptures exalt and rejoice over God's goodness and might, don't they?! Therefore, how will you plan to bless the Lord going forward?!

# DAY 2 – A DAY OF THANKSGIVING AND PRAISE

## QUESTIONS

1. Write out your blessings as they come to mind. Create a thank you list to God and include the following: 1. Everything you are thankful for, and 2. What He has done for you.

2. Did this day of thanksgiving make you feel closer to God? How?

3. What blessed you most today?

# 21 Day PRAYER CHALLENGE - DAY 2     Date:

_____

_____

_____

_____

_____

_____

_____

_____

_____

_____

_____

_____

_____

_____

_____

_____

_____

_____

# 21 Day PRAYER CHALLENGE - DAY 2    Date:

_____

_____

_____

_____

_____

_____

_____

_____

_____

_____

_____

_____

_____

_____

_____

_____

# 21 Day PRAYER CHALLENGE - DAY 2    Date:

_____

_____

_____

_____

_____

_____

_____

_____

_____

_____

_____

_____

_____

_____

_____

# 21 Day PRAYER CHALLENGE - DAY 2    Date:

_____

_____

_____

_____

_____

_____

_____

_____

_____

_____

_____

_____

_____

_____

_____

_____

Give thanks to the LORD, call on His name. Make known His deeds among the peoples; make them remember that His name is exalted.

Isaiah 12:4

# DAY 3 – A HEART TO HEART TALK WITH GOD

*Scripture – I Samuel 1:20, "And she was in bitterness of soul, and prayed to the Lord and wept in anguish."*

On this day before the Lord, during your time of prayer, have a heart-to-heart talk with your Heavenly Father. You can tell him exactly how you feel. Do not hold anything back. In the above scripture, Hannah prayed from her heart. She was distressed because she was unable to have a child and was ashamed. You see, in those days, it was a disgrace to not be able to give your husband a child. However, after Hannah had a heart-to-heart talk with God, she was able, by God's grace, to give birth to a child, and grant her husband an offspring. Be encouraged to be honest and transparent in your heart-to-heart talk with God today.

# DAY 3 – A HEART TO HEART TALK WITH GOD

## QUESTIONS

1. Journal a time that you were misunderstood because of the way that you felt. Eli the priest thought Hannah was drunk and rebuked her (I Samuel 1:14). God heard her heart and responded by granting her request (I Samuel 1:20).

2. What was your experience like when you had your heart-to-heart talk with God?

3. What blessed you most today?

# 21 Day PRAYER CHALLENGE - DAY 3    Date:

_____

_____

_____

_____

_____

_____

_____

_____

_____

_____

_____

_____

_____

_____

_____

_____

_____

# 21 Day PRAYER CHALLENGE - DAY 3    Date:

_____

_____

_____

_____

_____

_____

_____

_____

_____

_____

_____

_____

_____

_____

_____

_____

_____

# 21 Day PRAYER CHALLENGE - DAY 3    Date:

_____

_____

_____

_____

_____

_____

_____

_____

_____

_____

_____

_____

_____

_____

_____

_____

# 21 Day PRAYER CHALLENGE - DAY 3    Date:

_____

_____

_____

_____

_____

_____

_____

_____

_____

_____

_____

_____

_____

_____

_____

_____

_____

So I need to talk to you
And ask you for your
guidance
Especially today
When my life is so
cloudy
Guide me until I'm sure
I open up my heart.


Yolanda Adams

# DAY 4 – PRAY THE SCRIPTURE

*Scripture – I Corinthians 1:20, "For all the promises of God in Him are yes, and in Him Amen, to the glory of God through us."*

On this day before the Lord, during your time of prayer, incorporate scriptures. Praying the scriptures is very powerful, and it moves the heart of God. Some examples of scripture that you can speak forth during your prayer time are as follows: "You said in your word", (Matthew 24:35), "I believe your promises", (Philippians 4:19), "I'm standing on the word of truth", (Isaiah 55:11). Knowing scripture helps you to know God better. The more you get to know about God, the more you will trust Him.

# DAY 4 – PRAY THE SCRIPTURE

## QUESTIONS

1.In this journaling exercise, take the time to practice writing scriptural prayers that you can use in your prayer time. Use the examples above as your guide.

2.How did praying in this way help you?

3.What blessed you most today?

# 21 Day PRAYER CHALLENGE - DAY 4    Date:

_____

_____

_____

_____

_____

_____

_____

_____

_____

_____

_____

_____

_____

_____

_____

_____

_____

# 21 Day PRAYER CHALLENGE - DAY 4    Date:

_____

_____

_____

_____

_____

_____

_____

_____

_____

_____

_____

_____

_____

_____

_____

_____

_____

_____

# 21 Day PRAYER CHALLENGE - DAY 4     Date:

_____

_____

_____

_____

_____

_____

_____

_____

_____

_____

_____

_____

_____

_____

_____

_____

_____

# 21 Day PRAYER CHALLENGE - DAY 4    Date:

_____

_____

_____

_____

_____

_____

_____

_____

_____

_____

_____

_____

_____

_____

_____

_____

_____

No weapon that is formed against thee shall prosper; and every tongue that shall rise against thee in judgment thou shalt condemn. This is the heritage of the servants of the LORD, and their righteousness is of me, saith the LORD

Isaiah 54:17

# DAY 5 – SURRENDER IN PRAYER

*Scripture – James 4:10, "Humble yourselves before the Lord, and he will exalt you."*

On this fifth day before the Lord, during your time of prayer, surrender all to God. For the most part, we do not have a problem surrendering our problems, worries, and cares to the Lord. When it comes down to our will, what we want and desire does not always line up with God's wants and desires for us. We have to make sure that we are purposely surrendering ourselves to the Lord. Even Jesus had to say in Luke 22:42, "not my will but thy will be done." We have to take on the mindset of Christ and realize that we can do nothing of ourselves but we can do all things through Christ. Let us use our prayer time today to submit to God's wisdom.

# DAY 5 – SURRENDER IN PRAYER

## QUESTIONS

1.How are you submitting to God's ways by surrendering yourself to God?

2.Think of a time that you wanted something but you submitted to God's ways instead. Please share your experience.

3.What blessed you most today?

# 21 Day PRAYER CHALLENGE - DAY 5    Date:

_____

_____

_____

_____

_____

_____

_____

_____

_____

_____

_____

_____

_____

_____

_____

_____

# 21 Day PRAYER CHALLENGE - DAY 5    Date:

_____

_____

_____

_____

_____

_____

_____

_____

_____

_____

_____

_____

_____

_____

_____

_____

_____

# 21 Day PRAYER CHALLENGE - DAY 5    Date:

_____

_____

_____

_____

_____

_____

_____

_____

_____

_____

_____

_____

_____

_____

_____

_____

_____

# 21 Day PRAYER CHALLENGE - DAY 5    Date:

_____

_____

_____

_____

_____

_____

_____

_____

_____

_____

_____

_____

_____

_____

_____

_____

The Lord is my shepherd;
I shall not want. He
maketh me to lie down in
green pastures: he leadeth
me beside the still waters.
He restoreth my soul: he
leadeth me in the paths of
righteousness for his
name's sake.

Psalm 23:1-6

# DAY 6 – PRAY FOR YOUR ENEMIES

*Scripture – Matthew 5:44, "But I say to you, love your enemies, bless those who curse you, do good to those who hate you, and pray for those who spitefully use you and persecute you."*

On this sixth day before the Lord, during your time of prayer, pray for your enemies. By praying for your enemies, you are responding like the children of our heavenly father according to Matthew 5:45.  In fact, according to verse 46, we receive a reward when we learn to pray for our enemies. Another benefit we receive, based on verse 48, when we pray for our enemies, is that we reach perfection (maturity). You will therefore find it easier to forgive your enemies, and to keep your heart pure. Also, according to Romans 12:20, while you are praying for your enemies, you receive the blessing, but your enemies will have to deal with their guilt.

# DAY 6 – PRAY FOR YOUR ENEMIES

## QUESTIONS

1. After reading the scriptures below, how would you grade yourself on how you treat your enemies?

*Scripture readings: Exodus 23:5, "If you see the donkey of one who hates you fallen under its load, do not leave it there; you must help him with it." Proverbs 25:21, "If your enemy is hungry, give him food to eat, and if he is thirsty, give him water to drink."*

2. Now that you know what the word says about how to treat your enemies, how are you going to handle your enemies differently going forward?

3. What blessed you most today?

# 21 Day PRAYER CHALLENGE - DAY 6    Date:

_____

_____

_____

_____

_____

_____

_____

_____

_____

_____

_____

_____

_____

_____

_____

_____

_____

# 21 Day PRAYER CHALLENGE - DAY 6    Date:

_____

_____

_____

_____

_____

_____

_____

_____

_____

_____

_____

_____

_____

_____

_____

_____

_____

_____

# 21 Day PRAYER CHALLENGE - DAY 6    Date:

_____

_____

_____

_____

_____

_____

_____

_____

_____

_____

_____

_____

_____

_____

_____

_____

_____

_____

# 21 Day PRAYER CHALLENGE - DAY 6    Date:

_____

_____

_____

_____

_____

_____

_____

_____

_____

_____

_____

_____

_____

_____

_____

_____

_____

Spend a moment to pray for someone you are fighting with.

# DAY 7 – PRAY THE WILL OF GOD

*Scripture – Luke 22:42, "Saying, 'Father if you are willing, remove this cup from me. Nevertheless, not my will, but yours, be done."*

When Jesus prayed this prayer in the Garden of Gethsemane, He was overwhelmed with anguish and sorrow about what was before Him. Yet, He was able to surrender His will to God. Many times, when we come before God in prayer, we bring our own will to Him without even inquiring about His. However, Jesus completely placed God's will above his own in the Garden of Gethsemane. As a result, He entered a place of peace that truly 'surpassed all understanding.'

Today, as you seek God in prayer, come to Him with no agenda. Listen for His voice and pray what He speaks to you, according to His will. As you lean in further to His presence, keep your heart and mind open to the wisdom and insight He shares with you. After all, He knows the plans He has for you, and He desires what is best for you.

PEGGY RATLIFF

# DAY 7 – PRAY THE WILL OF GOD

## QUESTIONS

1.What did God reveal to you about His will for your life and/or a matter, or situation?

2.What response did you have towards God about what He shared?

3.What blessed you most today?

# 21 Day PRAYER CHALLENGE - DAY 7     Date:

_____

_____

_____

_____

_____

_____

_____

_____

_____

_____

_____

_____

_____

_____

_____

_____

_____

# 21 Day PRAYER CHALLENGE - DAY 7    Date:

_____

_____

_____

_____

_____

_____

_____

_____

_____

_____

_____

_____

_____

_____

_____

_____

_____

# 21 Day PRAYER CHALLENGE - DAY 7    Date:

_____

_____

_____

_____

_____

_____

_____

_____

_____

_____

_____

_____

_____

_____

_____

_____

# His will.
# His way.
# My faith.

# DAY 8 – A DAY OF REFLECTION

*Scripture – Psalm 95:6, "Oh come, let us worship and bow down; let us kneel before the Lord, our Maker!"*

There is no better place to be than in the presence of God! His love, goodness, and grace are unlike no other, and when we worship Him, we embrace the fullness of who He is, and enjoy Him! Worship also opens up our hearts to receive from God and to meditate on the things He has revealed to us.

As you spend time with God today, reflect on the things He has spoken to you thus far during the 21 Day Prayer Challenge. If you have taken any notes, you may want to review them during this time as well. Allow the Lord to lead you in this time of reflection, and share with you what is on His heart for you. Perhaps He may highlight an area to you that He wants you to work on, or an area that He wants to bring healing or empowerment to. Remember, the Lord is good, and His love endures forever; He withholds no good thing from those who walk uprightly.

PEGGY RATLIFF

# DAY 8 – A DAY OF REFLECTION

## QUESTIONS

1.What are 2-3 key things that came forth during your time of reflection?

2.What is one thing that you learned about you that was shared from God during your time of reflection?

3.What blessed you most today?

# 21 Day PRAYER CHALLENGE - DAY 8    Date:

_____

_____

_____

_____

_____

_____

_____

_____

_____

_____

_____

_____

_____

_____

_____

_____

_____

# 21 Day PRAYER CHALLENGE - DAY 8    Date:

_____

_____

_____

_____

_____

_____

_____

_____

_____

_____

_____

_____

_____

_____

_____

_____

_____

_____

# 21 Day PRAYER CHALLENGE - DAY 8     Date:

_____

_____

_____

_____

_____

_____

_____

_____

_____

_____

_____

_____

_____

_____

_____

_____

Live in such a way that those who know you but don't know God will come to know God because they know you.

H. David Burton

# DAY 9 – A DAY OF FASTING

*Scripture – Matthew 6:16-18, "When you fast, don't make yourselves look sad like the hypocrites. They put a look of suffering on their faces so that people will see they are fasting. The truth is, that's all the reward they will get. So, when you fast, wash your face and make yourself look nice. Then no one will know you are fasting, except your Father, who is with you even in private. He can see what is done in private, and he will reward you."*

Fasting is a personal and intimate response to God's instructions. It is an act, according to scripture, that is not to be done for "show and tell", but to be done in private. Some purposes of fasting are to strengthen prayer, to seek God's guidance, to seek deliverance or protection, and to express repentance and return to God. Fasting is also a beneficial and powerful tool of weaponry for us. Some benefits of fasting are that it causes us to depend on God, it helps us to bypass the emotions of our flesh, and increase our capacity to operate in the fruits of the Spirit, it opens our hearts to hearing God's voice, and it gives power to our prayers.

As you participate in this day of fasting, be expectant of miracles, healing, deliverance, growth, clarity, protection, and peace! Be encouraged that the turn around and/or breakthrough you desire will manifest in your life.

**PEGGY RATLIFF**

# DAY 9 – A DAY OF FASTING

## QUESTIONS

1.What was one change that you noticed in yourself or a situation during your fast?

2.Did you receive clarity and/or breakthrough for a situation, concern, or prayer request during your fast? If so, what happened?

3.What blessed you most today?

# 21 Day PRAYER CHALLENGE - DAY 9    Date:

_____

_____

_____

_____

_____

_____

_____

_____

_____

_____

_____

_____

_____

_____

_____

_____

# 21 Day PRAYER CHALLENGE - DAY 9    Date:

_____

_____

_____

_____

_____

_____

_____

_____

_____

_____

_____

_____

_____

_____

_____

_____

_____

# 21 Day PRAYER CHALLENGE - DAY 9    Date:

_____

_____

_____

_____

_____

_____

_____

_____

_____

_____

_____

_____

_____

_____

_____

_____

_____

_____

Fasting will loose the bands of wickedness, undo the heavy burdens, let the oppressed go free, and break every yoke.

Isaiah 58:6

# DAY 10 – A DAY OF LISTENING

*Scripture – Jeremiah 33:3, "Call to me and I will answer you, and will tell you great and hidden things that you have not known."*

There are many ways for us to seek God in order to listen to His voice. We can listen to His voice through prayer, fasting, speaking in tongues, worship/praise, and by reading His word, the Bible. We can also seek God in stillness and in quietness to listen to His voice.

Sometimes, however, this can be challenging with life's distractions, challenges, and busyness. We may even feel inept, on occasion, to set aside time much less be still long enough to listen to God's voice. We can rest assured though, that when we call to God, He will answer us, even IF it's in the midst of a storm, chaos, or uncertainty!

Today, as you seek God to listen to His voice, be open and expectant as to what God will share. Be ready to not only hear God's voice, but to also receive His instruction for what you need.

**PEGGY RATLIFF**

# DAY 10 – A DAY OF LISTENING

## QUESTIONS

1.What was one thing the Lord shared with you?

2.Did you hear anything from God that surprised you? If so, what was it?

3.What blessed you most today?

# 21 Day PRAYER CHALLENGE - DAY 10   Date:

_____

_____

_____

_____

_____

_____

_____

_____

_____

_____

_____

_____

_____

_____

_____

_____

_____

# 21 Day PRAYER CHALLENGE - DAY 10   Date:

_____

_____

_____

_____

_____

_____

_____

_____

_____

_____

_____

_____

_____

_____

_____

_____

# 21 Day PRAYER CHALLENGE - DAY 10   Date:

_____

_____

_____

_____

_____

_____

_____

_____

_____

_____

_____

_____

_____

_____

_____

_____

_____

_____

Don't let the noise of the world keep you from hearing the voice of God.

# HOW GOD CHALLENGES THE BELIEVER, AND WHY...

We rejoice in our sufferings because suffering produces endurance. Romans 5:3

PEGGY RATLIFF

# HOW GOD CHALLENGES THE BELIEVER, AND WHY...

The following are ways that you may be challenged as a believer:

- Testing of faith.
- Strengthening trust.
- Growth and maturity.

**PEGGY RATLIFF**

# HOW GOD CHALLENGES THE BELIEVER, AND WHY...

## Testing of faith...

Count it all joy, my brothers, when you meet trials of various kinds, for you know that the testing of your faith produces steadfastness. And let steadfastness have its full effect, that you may be perfect and complete, lacking in nothing. James 1:2

God may allow difficult circumstances to arise in a believer's life to **test their faith** and to help them grow in their relationship with Him. This kind of testing of our faith also develops character traits within us such as patience, perseverance, and humility.

**PEGGY RATLIFF**

# HOW GOD CHALLENGES THE BELIEVER, AND WHY...

**Strengthening trust...**

"Lord, if it is You," Peter replied, "command me to come to You on the water." Matthew 14:28

God may challenge us to step out in faith and trust Him in a new and unfamiliar way. This can lead to increased trust and dependence on Him. If we are never challenged, we will never grow and learn to depend on and **trust** in our heavenly Father. Challenges do serve to **strengthen** us and refine us. Refine means to go under fire, or to go under trial, or to confirm or strengthen who we are in God.

PEGGY RATLIFF

# HOW GOD CHALLENGES THE BELIEVER, AND WHY...

**Growth and maturity...**

You have been believers so long now that you ought to be teaching others. Instead, you need someone to teach you again the basic things about God's word. You are like babies who need milk and cannot eat solid food. For everyone who lives on milk is still an infant, inexperienced in the message of righteousness. Hebrews 5:12

God may challenge a believer, by encouraging them to **grow** and **mature** in their spiritual walk, through deepening their understanding of His word. It is through our challenges that we begin to mature and grow, and it is also the way that God operates in and through our lives. Never miss an opportunity, when challenged, to learn from it and to grow in your relationship with God as a result of it.

PEGGY RATLIFF

**Date:**

_____

_____

_____

_____

_____

_____

_____

_____

_____

_____

_____

_____

_____

_____

_____

_____

# 21 Day PRAYER CHALLENGE - REFLECTIONS

## Date:

_____

_____

_____

_____

_____

_____

_____

_____

_____

_____

_____

_____

_____

_____

_____

_____

_____

# 21 Day PRAYER CHALLENGE - REFLECTIONS          Date:

_____

_____

_____

_____

_____

_____

_____

_____

_____

_____

_____

_____

_____

_____

_____

_____

# 21 Day PRAYER CHALLENGE - REFLECTIONS

**Date:**

_____

_____

_____

_____

_____

_____

_____

_____

_____

_____

_____

_____

_____

_____

_____

_____

_____

_____

# DAY 11 – A DAY OF FAITH

*Scripture – Romans 10:17, "Faith comes by hearing, and hearing by the Word of God."*

God says, "If you have faith as small as a mustard seed, you can say to this mountain, 'Move from here to there,' and it will move. Nothing will be impossible for you." (Matthew 17:20-21) Are there any mountains in your life that you're currently facing? Or, are there any giants in your promised land (a place of blessings, promises fulfilled, etc.) that you are currently confronting? Faith is believing for something that is not yet visible in your life, and hoping for what you're believing to manifest tangibly in your life.

As we approach this day of faith, may we be encouraged that we only need a tiny seed of belief to get our faith in motion! God will respond to our faith, and do exceedingly, abundantly above all we ask or think! Sometimes, it's a faith step to believe in what we've heard (through the Word of God), and then to apply that faith towards the thing, situation, or circumstance. Other times, it may be a faith step to believe that God heard our prayer, and that He is working things out for our benefit even though we do not see results, yet.

**PEGGY RATLIFF**

# DAY 11 – A DAY OF FAITH

## QUESTIONS

1. How did you exercise your faith today?

2. How did God stretch or adjust your understanding about faith?

3. What blessed you most today?

# 21 Day PRAYER CHALLENGE - DAY 11   Date:

_____

_____

_____

_____

_____

_____

_____

_____

_____

_____

_____

_____

_____

_____

_____

_____

# 21 Day PRAYER CHALLENGE - DAY 11   Date:

_____

_____

_____

_____

_____

_____

_____

_____

_____

_____

_____

_____

_____

_____

_____

_____

_____

_____

_____

# 21 Day PRAYER CHALLENGE - DAY 11   Date:

Keep the faith. Some of the most amazing things in life tend to happen right at the moment you're about to give up.

# DAY 12 – A DAY TO PRAY FOR OTHERS

*Scripture – I Timothy 2:1, "First of all, I ask that you pray for all people. Ask God to bless them and give them what they need. And give thanks."*

One way to cultivate our relationship and intimacy with God is to pray for others. This is also another way we can serve God and His kingdom. As His children, we understand and know the reason God sent His son, Jesus Christ, into the world; it was and is to bring salvation to others. We also understand the call of the 'Great Commission' upon our lives, which is to go and make disciples of all nations, and to baptize them in the name of the Father, Son, and Holy Spirit. We therefore have a great opportunity and responsibility to partner with God!

Today, as you pray for others, be empowered with the following: 1. You are in the best and most powerful position to help, support, and cover them. 2. You are able to partner with God and pray His will over their lives. 3. You are fulfilling God's mandate for you, and sowing seeds to reap a harvest!

PEGGY RATLIFF

# DAY 12 – A DAY TO PRAY FOR OTHERS

## QUESTIONS

1.How did praying for others impact you?

2.If praying for others is not something you have done before, or done often, how did this challenge you? What changes will you put in place going forward?

3.What blessed you most today?

# 21 Day PRAYER CHALLENGE - DAY 12   Date:

# 21 Day PRAYER CHALLENGE - DAY 12   Date:

_____

_____

_____

_____

_____

_____

_____

_____

_____

_____

_____

_____

_____

_____

_____

_____

_____

# 21 Day PRAYER CHALLENGE - DAY 12   Date:

_____

_____

_____

_____

_____

_____

_____

_____

_____

_____

_____

_____

_____

_____

_____

_____

When you pray for others, God listens to you and blesses them. So, when you are safe and happy, remember that someone is praying for you.

# DAY 13 – A DAY FOR CHANGE

*Scripture – Romans 12:2, "Don't change yourselves to be like the people of the world, but let God change you inside with a new way of thinking."*

Change can occur in many forms and in many ways. For example, a global occurrence can bring about changes in the world, or personal circumstances can bring about changes in our lives. Also, a birth of a child, a loss of a loved one, or a couple getting married can all bring about changes to us and for us.

The change that God speaks about in Romans 12:2 begins with you and I. God doesn't want us to change ourselves according to the world's way of changing. Instead, He wants to change us from within. When we allow His word to transform our thoughts, we will have a renewed mindset. Our perspectives will change too. As you pray for a day of change, remember these following song lyrics, "Something on the inside, working on the outside, oh what a change in my life!" True, effective, long-lasting change begins with you!

**PEGGY RATLIFF**

# DAY 13 – A DAY FOR CHANGE

## QUESTIONS

1.What were some changes or a change that God highlighted to you to make?

2.How will this change within you impact those around you?

3.What blessed you most today?

# 21 Day PRAYER CHALLENGE - DAY 13   Date:

# 21 Day PRAYER CHALLENGE - DAY 13   Date:

_____

_____

_____

_____

_____

_____

_____

_____

_____

_____

_____

_____

_____

_____

_____

_____

_____

# 21 Day PRAYER CHALLENGE - DAY 13   Date:

_____

_____

_____

_____

_____

_____

_____

_____

_____

_____

_____

_____

_____

_____

_____

_____

_____

_____

We don't change God's word, but God's word changes us.

PEGGY RATLIFF

# DAY 14 – DENOUNCING BAD HABITS

*Scripture – Proverbs 28:13, "He who conceals his sins doesn't prosper, but whoever confesses and renounces them finds mercy."*

How kind, merciful, and compassionate is our God! He is slow to anger, abounding in love, and concerned about every detail of our lives. In fact, we can say that He is a very invested and involved Father! Therefore, we do not need to fear God or to be ashamed to approach Him in our nakedness. Instead, we can humble ourselves before Him and confess our sins. He is an ever-present help in times of trouble, and draws Himself closer to us as we draw ourselves closer to Him.

Consider then, what does denouncing bad habits look like for you? What do you need to destroy? Overspending? Watching too much T.V.? Spending too much time on social media? Perfectionism? Smoking? Unhealthy eating? Not getting enough exercise? During your time of prayer today, allow God to have "all access" to you. "I am confident of this, that the one who began a good work among you will bring it to completion by the day of Jesus Christ" (Phil. 1:6)

# DAY 14 – DENOUNCING BAD HABITS

## QUESTIONS

1.What were some of the roots or a root that God revealed to you that was the source of a bad habit (s)?

2.How did the Lord comfort you, or strengthen you, or bring healing to you?

3.What blessed you most today?

# 21 Day PRAYER CHALLENGE - DAY 14   Date:

_____

_____

_____

_____

_____

_____

_____

_____

_____

_____

_____

_____

_____

_____

_____

_____

_____

_____

# 21 Day PRAYER CHALLENGE - DAY 14   Date:

_____

_____

_____

_____

_____

_____

_____

_____

_____

_____

_____

_____

_____

_____

_____

_____

_____

_____

# 21 Day PRAYER CHALLENGE - DAY 14   Date:

_____

_____

_____

_____

_____

_____

_____

_____

_____

_____

_____

_____

_____

_____

_____

_____

To change your
life, change your
habits.

# DAY 15 – PEOPLE YOU NEED TO RELEASE

*Scripture – Ephesians 4:32, "Be kind and compassionate to one another, forgiving each other, just as in Christ, God has forgiven you."*

The definition of release is to allow or enable to escape from confinement; set free. When we consider the people that we need to release from our souls (heart, mind, emotions), we are inviting a freedom into our lives. This freedom delivers us from any pinned-up emotions or bondage that we were a prisoner to. This freedom also leads to a deeper healing. How? The truth sets us free! The truth may also hurt though as it's confronting the lie, or deception (blindness) that we were bound to. However, be encouraged beloved; it's the beginning of breakthrough!

As you seek God in prayer today regarding the people you need to release, know that "it is for freedom that Christ has set you free. Stand firm therefore, and do not submit again to a yoke of slavery." Galatians 5:1

# DAY 15 – PEOPLE YOU NEED TO RELEASE

## QUESTIONS

1. How did releasing people from your soul impact you?

2. How did the Lord comfort you, or strengthen you, or bring healing to you?

3. What blessed you most today?

# 21 Day PRAYER CHALLENGE - DAY 15   Date:

_____

_____

_____

_____

_____

_____

_____

_____

_____

_____

_____

_____

_____

_____

_____

_____

# 21 Day PRAYER CHALLENGE - DAY 15   Date:

_____

_____

_____

_____

_____

_____

_____

_____

_____

_____

_____

_____

_____

_____

_____

_____

_____

# 21 Day PRAYER CHALLENGE - DAY 15   Date:

_____

_____

_____

_____

_____

_____

_____

_____

_____

_____

_____

_____

_____

_____

_____

_____

_____

Forgive people in your life, even those who are not sorry for their actions. Holding on to anger hurts you, not them.

# DAY 16 – WATCH YOUR WORDS

*Scripture – Proverbs 18:21, "Death and life are in the power of the tongue."*

Our world was created by words. According to Genesis 1:3 it says, "Then God said, 'Let there be light!' And light began to shine." As children of God, we too have the ability to create our surroundings, our world, or our outlook on life or a situation based on the words we choose. How is that? We have God's spirit, the Holy Spirit, living within us and therefore are able to do what our Father does! So, imagine then how powerful our words are when we use them.

In your time of prayer, reflect on your recent word-choices, and ask the Holy Spirit to reveal how your negative words overpower your positive words that you may have spoken. Be encouraged as to what God will share with you.

**PEGGY RATLIFF**

# DAY 16 – WATCH YOUR WORDS

## QUESTIONS

1.What were two or three things God revealed to you about your words?

2.What new insight, or affirmation, or correction did God reveal and/or share with you?

3.What blessed you most today?

# 21 Day PRAYER CHALLENGE - DAY 16   Date:

_____

_____

_____

_____

_____

_____

_____

_____

_____

_____

_____

_____

_____

_____

_____

_____

_____

_____

_____

_____

# 21 Day PRAYER CHALLENGE - DAY 16   Date:

_____

_____

_____

_____

_____

_____

_____

_____

_____

_____

_____

_____

_____

_____

_____

_____

# 21 Day PRAYER CHALLENGE - DAY 16   Date:

_____

_____

_____

_____

_____

_____

_____

_____

_____

_____

_____

_____

_____

_____

_____

_____

_____

Watch your thoughts; they become words. Watch your words; they become actions. Watch your actions; they become habits. Watch your habits; they become character. Watch your character; it becomes your destiny.

Frank Jackson

# DAY 17 – ASK GOD FOR MORE

*Scripture – John 15:7, "If you abide in me, and my words abide in you, ask whatever you wish, and it will be done for you."*

In scripture, God encourages His people to ask Him for "whatever you wish, and it will be done for you." However, receiving whatever we wish for from God does not work like a genie in a lantern, whereby we make three wishes and instantly have what we asked for.

The key ingredients to having "whatever you wish done for you" is IF you abide in Christ, and His words abide in you. In other words, do you have relationship, fellowship, and covenant with God? Does His life reside in you? If yes, then whatever you ask for that is in accordance with God's will, you shall receive. You may not receive what you ask for in the way you thought or in the timing you desired, but rest assured you can ask God for more!

Be encouraged during your prayer time to seek and pursue God about the things of His kingdom, and to ask Him for more!

PEGGY RATLIFF

# DAY 17 – ASK GOD FOR MORE

## QUESTIONS

1.God wants us to come to Him with child-like faith. How did this encourage you to ask God for more?

2.What was one thing that you asked God for more of?

3.What blessed you most today?

# 21 Day PRAYER CHALLENGE - DAY 17   Date:

# 21 Day PRAYER CHALLENGE - DAY 17   Date:

_____
_____
_____
_____
_____
_____
_____
_____
_____
_____
_____
_____
_____
_____
_____
_____
_____
_____
_____

# 21 Day PRAYER CHALLENGE - DAY 17   Date:

# 21 Day PRAYER CHALLENGE - DAY 17   Date:

_____

_____

_____

_____

_____

_____

_____

_____

_____

_____

_____

_____

_____

_____

_____

_____

_____

_____

Seek God.
Trust God.
Praise God.

# DAY 18 – WHAT'S BLOCKING YOUR BLESSING?

*Scripture – Isaiah 48:17, "I am the Lord your God, who teaches you to benefit, Who leads you in the way you should go."*

There could be many factors that can block a person's blessings. Some examples are as follows: disobedience, unbelief, unforgiveness, pride, and rebellion. These blessing blockers are contrary to the fruits of the Spirit such as joy, peace, love, kindness, and faithfulness. Therefore, they block the presence of God in our lives and the flow of His spirit through our lives.

Have you been waiting for God's blessings to come forth in your life? Have you been believing God for what feels like overdue blessings? Do not lose hope in the wait, or feel faint in the wilderness because you feel like you have been forgotten. God is not like man that He should lie. He is not human, so he does not change His mind. Has He ever spoken and failed to act? Has He ever promised and not carried it through? (Numbers 23:19) So, today, during your prayer time, approach God's throne of grace with confidence and ask Him if there is anything that is blocking your blessing (s). Know that once you ask, He will answer. Be ready to receive His wisdom and insight.

PEGGY RATLIFF

# DAY 18 – WHAT'S BLOCKING YOUR BLESSING?

## QUESTIONS

1.What did God reveal to you about any blessing blockers in your life?

2.How were you encouraged to make amends with what God shared with you?

3.What blessed you most today?

# 21 Day PRAYER CHALLENGE - DAY 18   Date:

_____

_____

_____

_____

_____

_____

_____

_____

_____

_____

_____

_____

_____

_____

_____

_____

_____

# 21 Day PRAYER CHALLENGE - DAY 18   Date:

_____

_____

_____

_____

_____

_____

_____

_____

_____

_____

_____

_____

_____

_____

_____

_____

# 21 Day PRAYER CHALLENGE - DAY 18   Date:

_____

_____

_____

_____

_____

_____

_____

_____

_____

_____

_____

_____

_____

_____

_____

_____

_____

_____

# 21 Day PRAYER CHALLENGE - DAY 18   Date:

_____

_____

_____

_____

_____

_____

_____

_____

_____

_____

_____

_____

_____

_____

_____

_____

_____

Let God work. Don't block your blessings by moving too fast. When God is working on your behalf, be patient! Good things take time! Don't get weary, and don't get in the way!

# DAY 19 – A CHALLENGE TO STUDY MORE

*Scripture – Hosea 4:6, "My people are destroyed for lack of knowledge (of My law, where I reveal my will).*

Sometimes, we can have a tendency to interpret this scripture of Hosea 4:6 from a legalistic standpoint: "You better study more because you're a Christian and that's what you're supposed to do!" This narrative may have been passed down from religious and traditional mindsets, and could therefore be a discouragement and/or turn off for many people. After all, who wants to study more about God when it's being communicated like it's a chore? Or a strict rule? Where's the joy in that?

Our God invites us to walk with Him in grace, love, fellowship and peace. He longs to be gracious to us and rises to show us compassion. He wants to have an intimate relationship with us, and desires for us to draw close to Him. Now, doesn't this sound more inviting? In order for us to know our God, His ways, our inheritances, and the power and authority we carry, we need to read His manual! This manual, known as the Bible and God's word, gives us vision, wisdom, and understanding about WHO we are, WHOSE we are, and WHO we serve. Yet, if we don't dive into this rich context, how will we truly know these things? Before you know it, we could become victim to deception, blindness, and our rights as His sons and daughters, all because we simply don't know Him and His will well.

So, as you seek God today during your prayer time, study His word to show yourself approved! (II Timothy 2:15)

**PEGGY RATLIFF**

# DAY 19 – A CHALLENGE TO STUDY MORE

## QUESTIONS

1.What was one new thing that you learned about from reading the Bible?

2.What deeper insight or revelation did God show you about Himself or while reading the Bible?

3.What blessed you most today?

# 21 Day PRAYER CHALLENGE - DAY 19   Date:

_____

_____

_____

_____

_____

_____

_____

_____

_____

_____

_____

_____

_____

_____

_____

_____

_____

_____

# 21 Day PRAYER CHALLENGE - DAY 19   Date:

_____

_____

_____

_____

_____

_____

_____

_____

_____

_____

_____

_____

_____

_____

_____

_____

_____

_____

# 21 Day PRAYER CHALLENGE - DAY 19   Date:

_____

_____

_____

_____

_____

_____

_____

_____

_____

_____

_____

_____

_____

_____

_____

# 21 Day PRAYER CHALLENGE - DAY 19   Date:

_____

_____

_____

_____

_____

_____

_____

_____

_____

_____

_____

_____

_____

_____

_____

_____

_____

_____

If you don't have time to pray and read scriptures, you are busier than God ever intended you to be.

Matthew Kelly

# DAY 20 – A DAY OF TESTIMONY

*Scripture – Revelation 12:11, "And they overcame him by the blood of the Lamb, and by the word of their testimony."*

Our testimonies are actual evidence of God's miraculous and wonder working power within us. It is because of Jesus Christ's blood that we have been redeemed and restored! Our pasts no longer have control nor rights to haunt, taunt, and/or condemn us. We can therefore stand with our shoulders square, our heads upright, and with full confidence that we are not only the redeemed of the Lord, but we are also joint heirs with Christ! We are His sons and daughters!

Represent well then what God has done in and through you because of His son, Jesus Christ. Seek opportunities to boast to others of God's goodness, love, grace, and mercy in your life. Rise to the occasion to share with others that nothing is impossible for God! He can change their lives just like He changed yours! As you seek God in your prayer time today, be open and obedient to how God would like to use you as His billboard of transformation and grace!

**PEGGY RATLIFF**

# DAY 20 – A DAY OF TESTIMONY

## QUESTIONS

1. What was your day of testimony like? What experience or experiences did you have?

2. What is one thing you learned about the importance of sharing your testimony?

3. What blessed you most today?

# 21 Day PRAYER CHALLENGE - DAY 20   Date:

_____

_____

_____

_____

_____

_____

_____

_____

_____

_____

_____

_____

_____

_____

_____

_____

_____

_____

_____

# 21 Day PRAYER CHALLENGE - DAY 20   Date:

# 21 Day PRAYER CHALLENGE - DAY 20   Date:

_____

_____

_____

_____

_____

_____

_____

_____

_____

_____

_____

_____

_____

_____

_____

_____

_____

_____

# 21 Day PRAYER CHALLENGE - DAY 20   Date:

_____

_____

_____

_____

_____

_____

_____

_____

_____

_____

_____

_____

_____

_____

_____

_____

Your story is the key
that can unlock
someone else's prison.
Share your testimony.

# DAY 21 – A DAY OF REFLECTION

*Scripture – Psalm 95:6, "Oh come, let us worship and bow down; let us kneel before the Lord, our Maker!"*

There is no better place to be than in the presence of God! His love, goodness, and grace are unlike no other, and when we worship Him, we embrace the fullness of who He is, and enjoy Him! Worship also opens up our hearts to receive from God and to meditate on the things He has revealed to us.

As you spend time with God today, reflect on the things He has spoken to you during the 21 Day Prayer Challenge. If you have taken any notes, you may want to review them during this time as well. Allow the Lord to lead you in this time of reflection, and share with you what is on His heart for you. Perhaps He may highlight an area to you that He wants you to work on, or an area that He wants to bring healing or empowerment to. Remember, the Lord is good, and His love endures forever; He withholds no good thing from those who walk uprightly.

**PEGGY RATLIFF**

# DAY 21 – A DAY OF REFLECTION

## QUESTIONS

1.What are 2-3 key things that came forth during your time of reflection?

2.What steps will you apply to yourself as it relates to doing things God's way?

3.What blessed you most today?

# 21 Day PRAYER CHALLENGE - DAY 21   Date:

_____

_____

_____

_____

_____

_____

_____

_____

_____

_____

_____

_____

_____

_____

_____

# 21 Day PRAYER CHALLENGE - DAY 21   Date:

_____

_____

_____

_____

_____

_____

_____

_____

_____

_____

_____

_____

_____

_____

_____

_____

_____

_____

_____

# 21 Day PRAYER CHALLENGE - DAY 21   Date:

_____

_____

_____

_____

_____

_____

_____

_____

_____

_____

_____

_____

_____

_____

_____

_____

_____

Reflection. Looking back so that the view looking forward is even clearer.

*Blessings to you!*

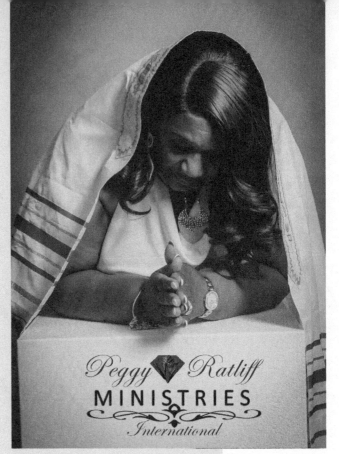

TO STAY CONNECTED WITH APOSTLE PEGGY RATLIFF, AND/OR FOR MORE INFORMATION ABOUT PEGGY RATLIFF MINISTRIES AND ADDITIONAL RESOURCES, PLEASE VISIT THE **CONTACT INFORMATION** BELOW!

# APOSTLE PEGGY RATLIFF
## www.peggyratliff.org

# CONTACT

- APOSTPEGGYRATLIFF
- PASTORPEGGYR
- TIKTOK@APOSTPEGGYRATLIFF
- TWITTER@RATLIFFPEGGY

Made in the USA
Monee, IL
07 June 2023